JEAN CASSOU

THE MADNESS
OF AMADIS

and other poems

Introduced and Translated by
TIMOTHY ADÈS

With a Foreword by
HARRY GUEST

AGENDA EDITIONS

First published in 2008 by Agenda Editions,
The Wheelwrights, Fletching Street,
Mayfield, East Sussex TN20 6TL

ISBN 978–0–902400–88–7

Thanks are due to © Éditions Gallimard, Paris, for *La Folie d'Amadis*
and *Une Rose s'est Noyée*, and to © Mme Isabelle Jan in respect of the
remaining poems.

Contents

Foreword by Harry Guest

Introduction: Jean Cassou: Amadis, Prince of Gaul

Notes to Other Poems – A Short Bibliography

Foreword by Harry Guest

The French, despite their self-induced reputation for fierce individuality, take comfort in forming -isms, counter-schools and splinter-groups. Only a Frenchman like Breton could actually have set up hard-and-fast rules for an anarchic movement like Surrealism.

Jean Cassou seems to have been his own man – purest of poets, an internationalist, more interested in literature and the visual arts than the temporary swirl of politics or jealous squabbles among myopic writers.

Labels such as 'baroque', 'romantic' or 'neo-classical' are useful for teachers and their pupils, but creative artists tend to slip out from the cage of identification. Beethoven, endlessly exploring ways of twisting music into fresh modes of expression, is neither wholly 'classical' nor 'romantic' – but, simply, Beethoven. Certainly, most major writers have surprised us by choosing the apparently untypical. Ronsard, supreme sonneteer, began an epic. Corneille, before embarking on those coldly passionate tragedies, produced *L'Illusion Comique* in which he undermined the very nature of drama. Musset, as well as lachrymose poems and beautiful plays to be enjoyed privately, produced a nonsense-satire in *Histoire d'un Merle Blanc*. Hugo's coruscating *Chansons des Rues et des Bois* delight us with their apparent casualness. Those who basked under Verlaine's rather mawkish moonlights may have been disconcerted by the obscene preoccupations of his 'zutiste' phase. None could have foreseen the limpid 'classicism' of *Clair-Obscur* when Cocteau exploded *Le Cap de Bonne-Espérance* during the First World War.

The only solution is to assess the entire oeuvre and accept that the process of living means alteration, shock, ripening, grievance, regret, consolation in unequal proportions. Any human seismograph can hardly avoid dreams, disappointments or epiphanies hovering round the next corner.

Nearly ten years after the magnificent 33 sonnets composed in captivity (radiantly translated by Timothy Adès in 2002) Cassou's contemporaries may have been surprised to discover in *La Folie d'Amadis* a serene withdrawal to the past. With its stately strophes rhymed *ababa* (with one crucial verse of six lines when Amadis meets the shepherds) we follow a beautiful pilgrimage of abandonment and re-discovery. The poem is, of course, a twentieth-century enterprise; the Alexandrines are frequently free

> *Se défaire en se perpétuant, belle histoire*

and the rhymes often flout classical rules (*fer / chimère*) but Cassou returns here to his first loves and feels delightedly at home in the lost world of medieval romance. As elsewhere, he coins memorably surrealist sentences like 'les cinq sens ont rendu leurs costumes de fête' and makes us experience in shorthand a Proustian moment when he describes 'une odeur mouillée / de livres lus enfant au paradis perdu'. Adès chose the dancing anapaests used by Byron for *The Destruction of Sennacherib* and these carry the narrative along effectively. If this technique lifts the poem slightly into an earlier form than the more modern encapsulation Cassou selected, this is all to the good as it subtly emphasises the French poet's fond glance at what he has inherited.

The other poems Adès includes in this fascinating selection vary in form but never in quality. The very title *Monsieur Alibi* whets the reader's appetite and we go on to find 'Il cherche un refuge dans le giron de la peur'. A morning is described as 'clair comme le cri d'une joueuse de tennis'. The powerful *Triomphe* contains a warning: 'tu interrogeras en vain la mémoire de la mer' and 'un feuillage de luths' is made to shiver. In *Campagne de Schiste* a sun has reindeer's horns. The quiet though spooky meditation on a wicker chair informs us that 'la misère… est ligotée comme une momie qui serait l'univers' and we are informed about 'un langage noir'. Cassou can convey desolation so deftly: 'Nos destinées sont des baisers évanouis'. In *1940* the sound of a bell can resemble 'un cri de noyé' as France sinks beneath the tide of invasion. The magnificent *Mémoire Longue* (which Adès rightly describes as one of Cassou's 'more desolate visions') offers, after hinting at curfew, shipwreck and exile, the chilling indication that 'tout le lendemain… est un rien'. *Voyageur, Je Te Conseille* – like a fantasy by Calvino – guides you through an invented city to a place where you will find 'ton plus cher et triste souvenir'.

While in prison – when his captors finally allowed him to read – Cassou chose a volume of Latin poetry. It is not surprising therefore that he chose themes like *Mars Émerveillé* and *Plaintes de Didon*, the latter a rich adaptation of a passage in Book IV of *The Aeneid* when the Queen of Carthage curses her fleeing lover, described as a 'ravisseur de pensées' as he heads for 'un horizon d'implacable mépris'.

Enfants Perdus is another major poem leaping from deliberately inappropriate colloquialisms to the bleakest humour in twists and turns of dazzling inventiveness where the décor includes 'une lampe à larmes de miel et de sang' and where 'un raccommodeur de vieilles pluies et d'éclairs cassés' passes by on the road, blowing his trumpet.

Cassou, an important though still somewhat under-appreciated poet, has been extremely fortunate in having once again Timothy Adès to translate his work. Adès has the enviable gift of lyrical lucidity. He captures the true heart of each poem he deals with and has the astonishing ability to follow the form of the original *exactly* in every conceivable way. Without ever sacrificing fidelity, never *replacing* the French text, he creates an entirely valid poem in English. 'Un saule défaillant' is 'a wrecked willow' and 'cette horreur parfaite' 'this zenith of dread'. 'Vie jouée, vie jugée' becomes 'a life was played, a life was weighed'; 'mes siècles toutes voiles dehors' turns validly into 'centuries that ran with all sails spread'; 'tristes cadeaux' are explained as 'sorry gifts'; 'canny' catches the quality of 'sensée'; 'vous voilà donc tombés au creux d'un somnambule / gouffre d'intemporalité' is brilliantly conveyed as 'You've fallen, I see, in the deep sleep-walk / in the chasm where time stands still'. 'Traînant son ballot de choses en retard' has almost a Beckettian flavour: 'dragging his bag of halts and hesitancies'. Adès's ear is impeccable: 'voleur de rien, trompeur pour rire' shifts into 'thief of nought, cheat for nought'; 'de structure funéraire' into 'built as if to mourn'; 'ce mystérieux élan au jarret' into 'that mysterious swing to their stride'. Two poems, especially, *Long Memory* and *Weak, So Weak*, are absolute models of excellence. Without strain, he creates a perfect mirror for Cassou's language:

> For all of the future that falls to my lot
> is a nil that is nil times none,
> at the price of privation and parent-loss,
> my real assets from this time on.

Personally, I am against facing pages of text. The eye is continually distracted away from the translation and the reader cannot properly appreciate either the French or the English. Better to read the French first, then hide the lefthand page and relish how Adès has coped so splendidly with the problem of 'making it new' in English while, incredibly, losing virtually nothing of the original quality. There is, alas, a fair amount of sloppy translation published nowadays, done by writers unskilled in prosody and, often, with a shaky control of the foreign language. That is why so scrupulous, so inventive, so professional, so poetic a translation as this one is so welcome.

Introduction

Jean Cassou

Jean Cassou is insufficiently recognised in France and abroad as a poet, let alone as a major cultural figure of his time. His famous *Thirty-Three Sonnets of the Resistance* have already appeared in English; this volume follows up with *The Madness of Amadis, Triumph, Glorious Romería*, and several shorter poems.

Jean Cassou, 1897-1986, the creator of France's National Museum of Modern Art, was for decades at the centre of cultural life in France and beyond. Art critic, poet, novelist, essayist, public figure, intellectual, man of action; imprisoned as a suspected Resistant; left for dead, his skull broken, at the liberation of Toulouse, 1944; he directed the Museum from 1949 to 1965 and was the main builder of its great collection, besides organising many exhibitions and writing copiously on art with great knowledge and insight. Always an outspoken public figure, he died loaded with honours.

Cassou was born at Deusto near Bilbao in Spain to a Spanish mother, an Andalucian, and his father's mother was Mexican; as a young man he translated Unamuno and Cervantes, and studied French and Spanish literature at the Sorbonne. After his father's death in 1913 he knew hard times. From the first he wrote about poetry as well as art (*Cubism and Poetry*, 1920): he was a co-founder of the journal *Nouvelles Littéraires*. Later he published *Three Poets*, a study of R.M. Rilke, Oscar Milosz and Antonio Machado.

The shock of the war and the Occupation made Jean Cassou himself a major poet. He moved south to the 'free zone' where he joined (and later led) the Resistance in Toulouse, and wrote a poetic sequence, *La Rose et le Vin*, completing it later with an extensive Commentary. He was arrested in late 1941 and held incommunicado in La Furgole prison, Toulouse; there, without pen and paper, he composed and memorised his famous *33 Sonnets Composés au Secret*. This literary classic was soon to be the first publication from Éditions de Minuit, with a magnificent introduction by Louis Aragon:

> 'He had no writing materials, this prisoner, save only time and his mental faculties. He had only the night for his ink, only memory for his paper. He had to hold the poem up, as one holds up a child out of the water. He had to hold it until the uncertain day of his release from prison. He had to do more than write it, he had to learn it.'

'From now on it will be almost impossible not to see in the sonnet the expression of freedom under constraint, the embodiment of thought in fetters.'

'And that poetry ... will certainly outlive all our prisons, just as the ebbing of a great flood leaves those thrilling messages at which children tremble in amazement, which register the level that was once attained, with the date: the high water mark of the great drama of France.'

In this first, clandestine edition, both men used assumed names, Jean Noir and François La Colère: John Black, Francis Anger. In peacetime the sonnets were translated, twice, into German. Much later, they were translated into English sonnets by Timothy Adès, and, along with much of Aragon's introduction and several of Cassou's other poems, were published bilingually by Arc Publications in 2002.

Cassou had not been badly treated in La Furgole prison. He had a lawyer; he was provisionally released, and later, he had a hearing. However, he was sentenced to a further year's detention, which he served in camps at Lodève and Mauzac, plus another month at St-Sulpice-la-Pointe. In June 1943 he was set free, and became leader of the Resistance in south-west France.

Liberation came to Toulouse on the night of 19-20 August 1944. That evening, Cassou, as regional Commissaire de la République, presided at a small meeting with the incoming mayor and others, preparing to take control. Leaving the meeting, their car, driven by a man wearing a tricolor armband with the cross of Lorraine, encountered the last German convoy. They were challenged, a pistol was found in the upholstery, they were severely beaten up. One man ran: he was hit by a bullet. Cassou was left in the road, his skull broken. After a long coma and many weeks of confusion, he had this to say:

'We've suffered. That's all I can tell you. I'm back from a strange journey. I must talk about those unknown lands. Beyond the cell there was something more! – there was death. I ventured into places where I left my companions behind. I fell bleeding on the streets of a great French city. For days and weeks I was in darkness. It's so easy to die, to be dead! When I awoke, France was free, the strict confinement was lifted. But the soul keeps its nocturnal habits. It takes a long time to re-train for the light. You have to set yourself again to affirm, to express, to speak, to see. To say yes to the world. Which we do. But you must grasp that we are coming from very far away.'

After the Liberation, Cassou was decorated by de Gaulle in his hospital bed. He became president of the National Writers' Committee, and of the Union of Intellectuals. But in 1949, when the Cominform condemned Tito for deviationism, and Laszlo Rajk was executed in Hungary, Cassou was one of the few prominent figures to break with the French Communist Party, which followed the Moscow line. For this he was vilified and deserted by most of his friends, though he attracted support from other quarters.

Amadis, Prince of Gaul

Cassou's poem 'The Madness of Amadis' appeared in 1950, in a small collection that included 'Schist Country', 'Dido's Reproaches', and 'The Poet's Winter':-

'He withdrew from his thoughts like wealth behind its windows and poverty in its doorway, like happiness in its goodbye.'

The resilient, positive tone of his war poems had ebbed away. His old physical injuries and the recent political brawls had pushed him back into himself, to draw deep on stories remembered from his childhood. Cassou's poem of Amadis resembles an antique ballad, although the resemblance is deceptive. Amadis, Prince of Gaul, is the hero of the most expansive and rambling of late medieval Spanish romances, the reading-matter that fuddled the brain of Don Quixote and was satirized by Cervantes. Books I-IV appeared by 1508, the named author being Garcí de Montalvo. One of the Conquistadores, Bernal Díaz, said that on their first sight of the Aztec capital city, Tenochtitlán (which became Mexico City), he was reminded of the enchanted cities in *Amadís*; and the name of California comes from the same romantic source. The text grew longer. *Amadís de Gaula* was translated, first into French, from 1540, then from French into English (1568; full text from 1589) and German, and on into Italian, Dutch and Hebrew. In the sixteenth and seventeenth centuries the saga was widely popular. Among English writers, Spenser, Sidney, Beaumont and Lyly all show the influence of Amadis.

Cassou's poem describes the fabled prince's retreat to wild places and the haunts of shepherds, his self-renewal, and the return to his love. The story as he tells it has no exact parallel in the original saga. There, early on, we find Amadis and Oriana in love-scenes, more restrained in the Spanish version than in the French. Already in Book I she weeps in her chamber for having unjustly accused him:

'Ah my eyes, no more eies but floods of tears!'

In Book II, jealousy drives the couple apart, and Amadis goes to be a hermit: he is close to death, and so is she. Even though it is not explicit, there must be a reconciliation, for in Book III they are together again. We find they are not just long-established lovers, but even have a child: two facts which, in their own courtly society, could never be admitted. In Book IV Oriana is respectfully told the duties of a princess.

Jean Cassou's version runs more or less concurrently with Books II to IV. It starts from the withdrawal of Amadis into a time and place of desolation, traces a time of his healing by the influence of nature and of ordinary people, and brings the couple together again. So, for all the apparent sadness of Cassou's poem, we have here the element of reconciliation that was missing from the old, convoluted story, and with it a happy ending.

La Folie d'Amadis

Amadis au tréfonds des forêts fait retraite.
À sa jument qui pleure il a donné congé,
baisant un dernier coup l'étoile de sa tête.
Puis, le col courbe sous sa crinière flammée,
elle s'est départie, blanche, vers d'autres quêtes.

Dispersée son armure aux échos du désert,
répudiés ses amis, rompu son train servile,
plantée sa croix d'estoc à l'ombre funéraire
d'un saule défaillant, il ressuscite, agile,
nu comme une âme, et bref, et libre à ciel ouvert.

« Ruisseau, dit-il, je suis ton pareil désormais,
digne de ton miroir évasif que les seules
faces des nymphes ont, fugaces, engravé.
De quel effacement le temps pur sous sa meule
nous procure l'aiguë et longue volupté!

Se défaire en se perpétuant, belle histoire.
C'est la nôtre, ami clair, mélodie que ma main
saisit et dont je veux emplir ma gorge noire
pour mieux l'entendre en moi me chanter mon destin
tout un jour sinueux jusqu'au gouffre du soir.

Musique, je me couche auprès de toi, parmi
les herbes humbles et les frêles fleurs qui penchent.
L'amour qui nous confond étend sur notre lit
un rideau verdoyant de frissons et de branches
que ne saurait percer nul rayon ennemi.

C'est moi qui, me dressant, irai chercher l'espace
à travers le feuillage, au fil de mon désir.
Tout est mien désormais: ma fortune, ma race,
le songe d'un épais et fatal avenir
où mon caprice étreint toute douleur qui passe,

The Madness of Amadis

He withdraws to the wildwood, the knight Amadis.
He sets free for a season his weeping white mare.
On the star of her forehead he plants a last kiss;
then she arches her neck with its flame-crest of hair,
and she canters away on adventures not his.

He has scattered his arms where the wilderness cries;
has rejected his friends; in the shadow of death
plants his sword like a cross, where a wrecked willow dies;
unattended, he gathers his poise and his breath;
bare and curt as a soul he stands free to the skies.

He says: 'Stream! now my lot shall be even as yours:
I am worthy your flickering glass, that alone
the nymphs' faces engraved in their fugitive hours.
Surely time in his mill grinds us small on the stone,
and a long and voluptuous sorrow is ours.

'It's by living for ever we fall in the fight:
that's our story, my friend, of that song I seize hold;
I shall gorge my black gullet, my comrade so bright;
I shall hear, deep within me, my destiny told,
through a sinuous day to the gulf of the night.

'Amid low-growing grass where the frail flowers lean,
hear me, Music! beside you my body I lay.
We shall mingle in love and be hid by a screen
that can never be pierced by an enemy ray,
a great curtain that shivers with branches of green.

'I shall rise up and go, I shall seek for that space,
passing through the green boughs by my bright thread of willing.
I'm master of all things: my fortune, my race,
and the dream of a future, a destined fulfilling,
where pain breathes its last in my fancy's embrace;

et le temps, mon temps universel, que d'ici
je contemple, astrologue au dos mélancolique,
ainsi qu'une planète en ses patients circuits.
Ma constance y poursuit d'une soif identique
un passé volontaire, un futur accompli.

Il ne m'est, pour tenir Oriane à moi nue,
que d'inscrire son nom de sang sur une écorce,
chiffre du souvenir, souffle du feu perdu,
beauté noyée, visage clos, cœur, cheveux, torse,
étincelants morceaux épars de ce qui fut.

Oriane, Oriane, ô richesse de l'âme,
abondance de grâce et de félicité,
fais ruisseler en moi l'effet de ton dictame,
fais toute mon intime harmonie expirer
dans le silence épanoui d'un nom de femme. »

Il dit, et par les rocs suit son pèlerinage.
Antres, pics et ravins, solitudes, absences
le regardent se perdre au creux le plus sauvage.
En ces extrémités la fureur de ses sens
s'apparie à l'effroi que versent les ombrages.

Là se dresse à ses yeux une géante pierre
bleue et plus déchirée qu'aucune vie humaine.
Roche-pauvre est son nom. Lui, de son maintien fier
la toisant, reconnaît que leur égale peine
le fait de ce royal charbon le juste frère.

'and of time universal, time present for me
that I scan like a planet so patiently turning,
a sad-backed astrologer, hunched with ennui;
and my constancy tracks with identical yearning
a chosen time past, an achieved time to be.

'To enfold Oriana's bare limbs within mine
I need write but her name on the bark of a tree:
breath of fire that has vanished, memorial-sign,
scattered sparks that are fragments of what used to be:
limbs, hair, heart, the closed face; the drowned beauty divine.

'Oriana! my lady, my soul's precious hoard,
O, the grace and well-being and joy that abound!
Oriana, your balm in my vessels is poured.
Let your silence extinguish my innermost sound:
it blooms bright in the name of a lady adored.'

So he spoke and, a pilgrim, he goes on his way.
Rocks and caverns and peaks and the parched solitude
see him enter a gully, stark, savage and grey.
In these desolate wastes his intemperate mood
matches well with the horrors such shadows display.

Now there rears up before him a towering stone:
it is blue, and more fissured than any man's life.
Call it Poverty Rock. All at once he has known,
proudly taking its measure of sorrow and strife,
that this monarch of crags is his brother, his own.

Même est leur droit, mêmes leur chair et leur nature.
Pourtant le cœur de l'homme est encor le plus fort.
Car la pierre est sans âge, et dure, elle perdure,
et le cœur, tressaillant aux blessures du corps,
s'enorgueillit de persister dans de l'usure.

Beau chevalier, beau ténébreux, roc de misère,
dépouillement d'un chêne, écorché dénuement,
il fallait t'en venir jusqu'a ce finistère
pour mesurer ta gloire et tout son monument
formé de l'abandon d'une existence entière.

Comme la mort est belle en cette horreur parfaite!
Comme la vie est vaste en cette gueuserie!
Les cinq sens ont rendu leurs costumes de fête.
Fermée, la bouche a fait ses adieux au mépris,
et le mépris, les poings liés, baisse la tête.

Un crépuscule noir saigne sur l'étendue.
L'heure s'arrête. Au fond monte une odeur mouillée
de livres lus enfant au paradis perdu,
et de recueillements sur l'épaule des fées,
et de soirs tout pareils, lointains et suspendus.

Un pas de plus, et les secrets vont s'entr'ouvrir,
corolles recélant les yeux à reconnaître.
Ô silence! un frisson avide d'en finir
présume l'éperdu bonheur de sentir naître
le point le plus subtil de l'instant de mourir.

Eh! quoi, serait-ce un mort, ce mannequin de fer
Qu'on a vu, fabuleux, vers les champs redescendre,
tendant un cœur spectral dans les doigts de chimère
du gant raide et portant la solennelle cendre
d'un astre consumé derrière sa visière?

They are equal in nature, in flesh, and in right;
for the stone is unheeding, and agelessly lasts:
yet the heart of a man is the stronger in might,
for the heart struggles on through the blows and the blasts
with the pride to persist in the fray and the fight.

Gallant knight of the shadows, you suffering stone,
naked trunk of an oak-tree, stripped down and bereaved,
you were drawn to come out to this desolate zone
to weigh up all your glory and all you achieved
when you left an existence, to journey alone.

O how lovely is death at this zenith of dread!
O how splendid is life in this beggarly place!
We renounce our fine clothes, the five senses have said,
and contempt is dismissed with a hard stony face,
and his wrists have been tied and he lowers his head.

Black twilight is bleeding, the minutes are ended;
the paradise lost when the children grow older,
damp smell of their story-books slowly ascended,
and comforting sprites when you cry on their shoulder,
and evenings, repeated, far off and suspended.

One more step and the secrets are sure to be known.
They are petals, behind which the eyes are unseeing.
O silence! a shudder that longs to have done
preconceives the deep joy when there comes into being
the delicate moment when life is foregone.

Human figure of steel! Is he one of the dead,
man of legend we saw to the meadows return,
with the heart of a ghost in a hand gauntleted,
a chimera who bears, in the funeral urn
of his visor, the ash of a star that is fled?

« Il est venu ce soir, m'ont conté les bergers.
Il a franchi tel un simple rayon de lune
nos échines en rond penchées sur le foyer.
Il a défait son casque et, sans parole aucune,
mangé de notre pain et vidé d'un long trait,
l'œil clos sur ses pensées, l'outre de cuir commune.

Nous regardions, béants, ce visage cireux
posé sur le tranchant de la cuirasse immense
comme un chef-reliquaire et l'émail précieux
des lèvres qui, soudain, brisèrent le silence
pour nous parler de nos travaux et de nos jeux.

Chacun de nous alors lui conta ses herbages,
tel ses moutons touffus, et tel autre l'osier
qu'il faut savoir tresser pour les claies des fromages.
Il répondait à tous et nous interrogeait.
Puis il s'en est allé vers le prochain village. »

Amadis a marché jusqu'au petit matin,
respirant le sommeil des hommes et des bêtes,
pressant contre son cœur l'agonisant parfum
de la folie dont il s'était donné la fête,
et son château s'est révélé, comme un destin.

Son énorme château surgissait. La muraille
ouvrait son flanc et lui tendait son pont-levis
comme la main lassée qu'un jour de funérailles
on offre à la pitié lugubre des amis.
Et tous les soupiraux crachaient leur valetaille.

Et dans la cour le revenant se vit, debout,
membres gourds sous l'acier, visage nu, la proie
des chiens et des parents qui lui sautaient au cou.
Sous les embrassements des monstres d'autrefois
il savoure à pleins bords l'extase du dégoût.

'He was with us this evening', the shepherds disclosed.
'He moved up like a moonbeam so easily there,
where we rounded our backs by the fire and reposed.
He unfastened his helmet, in silence, head bare;
freely ate of our bread; then he pondered, eyes closed,
and drank deep from the old leather bottle we share.

'His face was all waxen, and poised on the port
of his mighty cuirass, that with awe we beheld,
like a shrine; and his lips were enamel, well-wrought.
It was these broke the silence, abruptly dispelled,
when he asked how we fared, at our toil and our sport.

'There were answers aplenty to give and receive;
for each one of us told of our pasturing-places,
the wool-tufted sheep and the reeds that we weave
for enclosing the cheeses in wickerwork cases.
The next village beckoned; the prince took his leave.'

Amadis kept his course till the dawning of day,
breathing deep of the slumber of man and of beast,
and he pressed to his heart the tormenting bouquet
of the madness he'd tasted and had for a feast;
then his castle like destiny reared in his way.

His great castle rose up and the walls opened wide
at its flanks; the limp hand of a drawbridge was offered,
as if to the friends of a man who has died,
on the funeral day, for the grief they have suffered.
Through ports, the retainers came streaming outside.

So the prodigal stands in the courtyard at last,
limbs all numb in his armour, uncovered his face,
overwhelmed by the monsters who spring from the past,
prey of dogs and of kinsfolk who leap and embrace:
he drinks deep of the cup of ecstatic distaste.

Mais enfin secouant toute cette poussière
et levant les regards vers la vitre, là-haut,
il devine Oriane a l'attente derrière,
elle est là, il le sait, lourde, contre un rideau,
oisive dans le noir, telle une chambrière.

Il monte l'escalier, pousse la porte et dit:
« Dame, en ce revenir à tant de choses mortes
qu'il faut recommencer à vivre avec ennui,
c'est toi ma seule joie. Et moi, je te rapporte
cette tête plongée dans les eaux de la nuit. »

All this dust he shakes off: it is finally laid
and he raises his eyes to the windows above:
she is leaning, he knows it, against the brocade,
he can tell Oriana is waiting, his love,
in the dark of the room, like a loitering maid.

Up the stair, through the door he advanced and he said:
'O my lady, I come to my duty anew,
to the languor of life amid all that is dead.
You alone are my joy, I surrender to you,
though the waters of night had closed over my head.'

Autres Poèmes

Une Rose s'est Noyée

Une rose s'est noyée
dans une coupe de vin,
et, défaillante, effeuillée,
elle exhale son destin.

« Ô bonheur de mourir ivre!
Ô parfait contentement!
Dès mon aube je me livre
au plus âpre des amants.

Que bénie soit la main blanche
qui dans ce feu m'a jetée,
où, saisi, mon cœur épanche
le parfum qui lui restait!

Trop plus de sang m'environne,
trop plus de nuit éperdue,
que la soif qui m'abandonne
n'aurait jamais attendue.

Si le nœud de mes pétales
délivre enfin ses liens,
c'est que je suis assez pâle
pour ne plus paraître rien. »

Visage qui se consume
dans la transparence noire,
la fleur aux regards posthumes
n'est qu'un plaisir sans mémoire.

Other Poems

A Rose that was Drowning

A rose that was drowning
in wine in a bowl
all loosened and swooning
breathed out life and soul.

'O joy, drunken dying!
My cup runneth over!
Since my dawn I've been yielding
to an ungentle lover.

'I bless the white hand
threw me in the melting.
What perfume remained,
my heart spills, exulting.

'More deep the blood oozing,
more deep, night of passion,
than the thirst I am losing
could ever imagine.

'If the knot of my petals
may finally fall,
I'm so pale, I seem
to be nothing at all.'

The dark limpid liquor
her face must destroy:
death-gaze of the flower,
oblivious joy.

Cependant qui, de ses lèvres,
aspire cette agonie
croit en vain cueillir la fièvre
et les soupirs d'une amie.

Mais elle, rien que fondue
avec l'engloutissement
du désir qui la veut nue,
elle n'est, en ce moment,

que le seul amour qui l'aime,
cela même dont on meurt,
l'étendue à face humaine,
le cœur de l'autre, le cœur…

Yet he who aspires
to taste of this anguish
cannot sample her fires
though his lover may languish.

But she, simply foundered
in the drowning desire
that longs for her naked,
she now is no more

than the one love that loves him,
the love death must part,
the face on the surface,
the other's own heart ...

Triomphe

Cœur, ce cœur, que de secrets, que d'acerbes,
saignants, malodorants secrets aux fosses croupissaient
de ses fosses, la d'où ne remontait nulle herbe.

Mais là des poissons éteints, des serpents mordus
    s'entassaient
afin que ne fût connue, seule, en la région arpège,
que toi, la chronique d'ivoire qui transfigures les journées!

Cœur, le cœur enseveli suscite, à la façon des morts,
le poids vertical et de neige durcie du château,
la fontaine aux licornes et aux panthères, et les brumeux
    contreforts,

et la terrasse des anges. Or c'est plus haut encore que les
    créneaux,
dans le vitrage du vertige, miroir des beaux incendies du port,
qu'il faut lire l'histoire aux oiseaux.

Ils ne te demanderont que ton chant, les adorables. Donc oublie
la pourriture. Oh! je sais: dans le silence des cellules,
eux, ils reparaissaient, les pourrissants secrets, comme les mots
    se lient

l'un à l'autre, vertigineusement, dans un discours curule,
portant condamnation solennelle contre ta vie.
Car toute vie humaine est pareille à une vieille enfant ridicule.

Vie jouée, vie jugée, les passants la froissaient
comme un pied de fenouil pour lui faire rendre son odeur triste.
Nul recours quand tu te dandinais comme un écolier,

le pire, celui qui ne veut pas réciter l'histoire du Christ,
et quand tu t'acheminais vers ton obstination esseulée,
et quand, hurlant, Misère et Maladie flairaient ta piste.

Triumph

Heart, this heart, what secrets, what bitter secrets are those,
what bloody, stinking secrets were crouching in the ditches
of their ditches, from which no grass grows?

In them were heaped up bitten snakes and rotting fishes
so that nobody might be known, where the harp-ripple plays,
but you, the ivory chronicle, transfigurer of days.

Heart, the heart in grave-clothes raises as dead men do
the fountain of panthers and unicorns, and the misty counter-fort,
the vertical weight of the castle, the weight of hardened snow,

and the terrace of the angels. But it's higher than ramparts go,
in the vertiginous mirror that reflects the burning port,
that the tale must be read to the birds, the wren and crow.

They will ask for your song and nothing more, the dear ones. So
    forget
the putrescence. Oh! I know it: in the silence of the cells
they'll turn up, the rotting secrets, in the way that words connect

to each other, vertiginously, in a judgment that upheld
a solemn condemnation against the life you've led,
for every human life is like an old ridiculous child.

A life was played, a life was weighed, scrunched up by
    passers-by
like the end-stump of a fennel to yield its doleful smell.
No help for it when you toddled along like a small schoolboy,

the worst, the one unwilling to recite the gospel tale.
Alone, cast out, you headed off to your perversity,
while poverty and sickness were howling on your trail.

Les heures se mirent en marche comme un défilé de pages
portant haut clairons, corbeilles et flambeaux.
Comment oser en saisir une au passage?

Elles s'en furent vers la pinède raide au ras des flots
et glissèrent sans fin sur le pont arc-en-ciel. Et pour toi leur
    message
ne fut qu'un retentissement de silence dans l'ouïe d'un
    tombeau.

Comme le banquier sous l'œil anxieux de la ménagère
cherche à ses doigts la trace d'un tel écoulement d'or,
tu interrogeras en vain la mémoire de la mer

et tout cet ossuaire de paysages morts,
criant: « Mais où donc sont restés, sur quelles îles, quelles
    berges
mes journées, mes années, mes siècles toutes voiles dehors? »

C'est une surprise étrange, en vérité, que de ne plus savoir
compter, avec les nombres qu'apprennent les enfants,
les choses qu'on a possédées et ces feuilles noires

qui de notre calendrier intérieur se sont éparpillées au vent
l'une après l'autre comme une arithmétique avare,
et ta main creuse doit dire: « Je n'ai rien connu du temps. »

Est-il possible, cœur impur, de tirer un bien du mal?
Toi qui m'écoutes, sache que ta jeunesse est née dans une
    lande
vénéneuse où les pèlerins traînent un pas inégal,

et à travers cette nuit dont les terres déchirées s'étendent
tu parvins jusqu'où t'attendait la promesse du val,
là où siège la dame à la tunique bleu lavande,

The hours marched off, as a page-boys' procession might do,
with bugles, baskets and torch-lights all beautiful and brave.
How to be bold and seize an hour as they went marching through?

They headed for the pinewood that reared at the edge of the wave,
and slipped beneath the rainbow bridge, for ever. Their word to
   you
was only an echo of silence in the hearing of the grave.

As a banker, with his housekeeper watching anxiously,
searches his fingers for traces of so much gold mislaid,
you'll vex with futile questions the memory of the sea

and all that boneyard of countrysides long dead,
crying: 'What shores, what islands, have kept away from me
my days, years, centuries that ran with all sails spread?'

It's very strange to lose the skill, it certainly amazes,
of counting, with the numbers that children memorise,
the things we previously possessed, and those black leaves or
   pages

of our internal calendar that scattered to the skies,
one behind the other, and the tally was rapacious!
'I had no sense of Time', your empty hand must recognise.

Is it possible, impure heart, to wrest from the ill some good?
Know this, my listener: in a poisoned land you grew,
a land where the pilgrims drag an unequal tread.

You came where the promise of the vale awaited you,
across that night where the ragged lands are spread,
to the seat of the Lady in the tunic of lavender blue,

Dame Dialectique sur son trône de musée.
Son visage pareil à celui d'un cantique était sérieux
et innocent à la fois, et un air de petite fille sensée

allongeait ses mains dans les plis de sa robe et fixait ses yeux
sur les changements que savent opérer les fées
et que tu ne voyais point, toi qu'écrase un ciel malheureux.

Elle se leva, toute pure, et c'était aussi l'amour,
la dame d'amour qui donne un nom à chaque minute
et qui à chaque chose créée vient faire sa cour.

À son passage frémissait un feuillage de luths
et sur sa traîne veillait un cortège de chiens
qui semblaient devoir la préserver de toute chute,

des chiens beaux comme le jour et bons comme le bon pain,
et elle les caressait de sa main douce et elle disait:
« N'ayez pas peur. Approchez-vous. Ce n'est rien.

Ce n'est rien. Une pensée du cœur désespéré.
Une pensée qui restitue le monde, cœurs de petite foi.
Le réveil gît dans le songe et la trouvaille dans la chose
    cachée.

Dans les mystères de la faute sont le pardon et la joie. »
Alors tu te sentis gonflé de fleurs comme un matin de
    fiançailles,
tu relevas la tête et la regardas tout droit.

Mille autres voyageurs, avec toi, marchaient, vaille que vaille,
et vous tendiez vos goitres de stropiats affamés,
et vous pressiez vos ailerons pointus de mendiants qui
    défaillent,

et le sourire de la dame était beau comme une mort consolée.

Camp de Mauzac 1943 – Paris 1947

the Lady Dialectica, on her museum throne.
Her face was like the face of a canticle, it was
both innocent and earnest, and a canny young girl's tone

stretched her hands in her dress's folds and turned her eyes
toward the transformations the fairy-folk bring on.
You never saw it, you who are crushed by dismal skies.

She rose up, all purity, and she was love as well,
the queen of love, who welcomes every minute with a name,
the lover of created things, who visits one and all.

There was foliage of lutes that trembled as she came;
her dogs, whose task, it seemed, was to guard her from a fall,
made a close procession, keeping watch about her train:

her dogs were beautiful as day, and good as well-baked bread.
She stroked them with a gentle hand, and all the time she said:
'Come closer. It is nothing. No need to be afraid.

'Nothing at all. A thought when the heart despairs of love:
a thought that can restore the world, you hearts of little faith.
Waking lies dormant in dreaming, in the hidden lies treasure-
    trove.

'In the mysteries of error there is pardon, there is joy.'
You felt as if swollen with flowers, on the day you were betrothed:
you raised your head and looked her in the eye.

Walking beside you, come what may, journeyed a crowd untold,
and you offered up your goitres of the starving and the crippled,
you plied your pointed ailerons of beggars, sick, enfeebled,

and the lady's smile was beautiful as a death consoled.

Campagne de Schiste

Campagne de schiste sous un soleil aux cornes de renne.
La volonté du gros fleuve roux perce l'épaisseur.
Sanctifiée soit la volonté du fleuve.
Éparses, les autos, comme des boîtes de conserves, comme
    des crustacés de quartz,
scintillent dans l'aride immensité.
J'inscris ton œil sur l'os et le métal.
Sanctifiés soient les yeux, comme des cailloux, dans le sac
    de la vieille cribleuse.
Ils tomberont en pluie sur l'étendue
et feront naître une ville comme un pin parasol,
avec toutes ses familles.
Sanctifié soit ce qui sourd des profondeurs et s'allonge et
    absorbe ce qui piquait.
Un assouvissement d'orchestres embrasse le hérissement
    du sol.
Aux narines du ciel montent les senteurs du chevreuil
    minéralogique.
Mais sanctifié plus encore et par-dessus toute chose soit
    le silence qui sait.
Un enfant a mis un doigt sur sa bouche
et de l'autre main désigne la totalité.

Orgueil, Enfant Secret

Orgueil, enfant secret, enfant blessé, j'irai te voir
à l'heure de la visite. Je prendrai place, humblement,
dans la salle d'attente, auprès des gens qui seront là,
lourds d'oranges et de tristes cadeaux. Mais moi,
je ne t'apporterai que mes mains nues dans mes poches vides.
Et parvenu à ton chevet je pencherai sur toi des yeux sans
    larmes,
un regard fier et froid.

Schist Country

Schist country under a sun with reindeer horns.
The big red river's desire pierces the thickness.
Hallowed be the river's desire.
Scattered, the cars, like tinned food, like quartz crustaceans,
glitter in the arid immensity.
I inscribe your eye on the bone and the metal.
Hallowed be the eyes, like pebbles an old woman sifts in a bag.
They will fall like rain on the vastness
and give birth to a city like an umbrella-pine,
with all its families.
Hallowed be that which wells up from the depths, spreading,
    absorbing all irritations.
A gratification of orchestras embraces the bristling of the soil.
The mineralogical roebuck scent climbs to the sky's nostrils.
But hallowed still more and above all things be the knowing
    silence.
A child has put its finger to its mouth
and with its other hand describes totality.

Pride, Secret Child

Pride, secret child, wounded child, I shall go to see you
at visiting-time. I shall take my place, humbly,
in the waiting-room, among the people
heavy with oranges and sorry gifts. But I
shall bring you only my bare hands in my empty pockets.
And reaching your bedside I shall look at you dry-eyed,
my gaze proud and cold.

Une Chaise de Paille

Une chaise de paille au clair de lune et le silence
dans la chambre. On ne peut entrer ni sortir.
On ne peut que la misère. Elle est présente et ligotée
comme une momie qui serait l'univers.
Tu pleures? Il ne faut pas pleurer. Il faut, il faut
rentrer les pleurs au fond du caillou noir.
Homme stupide, cœur fixe, il faut t'en tenir à ta nuit
    de misère.
Et pas un muscle et pas un nerf ne tressailliront
    jamais plus,
ni cet infinitésimal déclic mouillé des paupières
qui jadis annonçait la naissance d'une chanson
dans les ténèbres du repos. Il ne faut plus jamais
    recommencer.
Il ne faut plus. Plus rien ne faut. Mais
le langage d'une mâchoire scellée dans la muraille
est un langage noir et qui doit plaire
à l'âme curieuse en ses festons de carnaval
et qui se penche comme une fille aux aguets. Elle sourit,
elle est flattée et bien contente. Elle repart
sur la pointe des pieds comme une qui pense
qu'avril va revenir avec ses fioritures. Pauvre âme!
Seuls, autour de leur feu, les dormeurs sauvages
tournent la tête. Et le feu lourd s'éteint.

A Wicker Chair

A wicker chair in the moonlight and silence
in the bedroom. No way one can enter or leave.
No way but poverty. Which is present and tightly wrapped
like a mummy that would be the universe.
You shed tears? You must not shed tears. You must, you must
send the shed tears back to the depths of the black stone.
Stupid man, heart unmoved, you must keep to your night of
    poverty.
And not a muscle and not a nerve will ever shake again,
nor that infinitesimal wet click of the eyelids
that once used to announce the birth of a song
in the shadows of rest. You must never start up again.
You must never. Never must anything. But
the language of a jaw sealed into the wall
is a dark language that must please
the curious soul in its carnival garlands
leaning forward like an attentive girl. She smiles,
flattered and very pleased. She sets off
on tiptoe like one who thinks
April will return with its blossoms. Poor soul!
Alone, round their fire, the wild sleepers
turn their heads. And the heavy fire goes out.

Monsieur Alibi

Le connaissez-vous? Non, vous ne le connaissez pas.
Seules, le connaissent la misère et la solitude, et aussi la peur
quand il cherche un refuge dans le giron de la peur.
Car la peur est comme une mère pour lui et comme les meubles
    de la chambre maternelle dans leur odeur de soir d'hiver.
Il est dans cette odeur, il est où vous n'avez jamais été.
Il est dans un métier très vil qu'il a fait autrefois, pour s'amuser
    sans doute.
Il est dans la rencontre d'une nuit de voyage et dans un baiser
    à jamais perdu.
Il est dans une matinée que nul n'a comprise et qui était là
    pourtant,
claire comme le cri d'une joueuse de tennis et couronnée
    d'irradiantes pervenches.
Il est dans une lointaine capitale, c'est la veille du départ, il se
    plonge une dernière fois dans la foule, regarde les vitrines
    et saigne d'une insolite mélancolie.
Il est au bras de ses compagnons d'orgie, l'un mort à vingt ans,
    l'autre dont il a oublié le visage, il les aime avec désespoir,
    il mêle son désespoir à leurs chansons d'ivrognes.
Il est dans un bureau, il commande et il obéit, un nom est
    inscrit sur sa porte.
Il est parmi de grands dangers et continue de marcher comme
    un promeneur.
Il est sous l'œil de son horoscope, et l'œil le suit comme un
    faisceau lumineux dans un dédale.

Monsieur Alibi est entré dans sa jeunesse.
Il y a retrouvé le caillou qu'il poussait du pied au jour de la plus
    affreuse détresse,
sur le chemin de cette gare de banlieue, et il faisait une chaleur
    hallucinante.
Monsieur Alibi est entré dans le caillou hallucinant.

Mr Alibi

Do you know him? No, you don't know him.
He is known only to poverty and loneliness, and also fear
when he looks for refuge in the bosom of fear.
For fear is like a mother to him and like the furniture of a
    mother's room that smells of a winter evening.
He is in that smell, he is where you have never been.
He is in a very low trade which he carried on in the past,
    doubtless for fun.
He is in a nocturnal encounter during a journey, in a kiss lost for
    ever.
He is in a matinée that nobody understood, yet it was there,
bright as a tennis-girl's shout and crowned with spokes of
    periwinkles.
He is in a distant capital, it's the day before he leaves, he takes
    one last plunge into the crowd, scans the shop-windows
    and bleeds with unaccustomed melancholy.
He is arm in arm with the companions of his orgies, this one
    died at twenty, that one's face he forgot, he loves them
    to despair, mingles his despair with their drunken songs.
He is in an office, he issues and obeys instructions, has a name
    on his door.
He is beset with perils and carries on walking as if out for a stroll.
He is under the eye of his horoscope, and the eye follows him
    like a light-pencil in a labyrinth.

Mr Alibi has gone into the days of his youth.
He has found the pebble he kicked on the day of grimmest
    distress,
on the road to that suburban station, and it was so hot, it was
    hallucinatory weather.
Mr Alibi has gone into the hallucinatory pebble.

Monsieur Alibi est entré dans les ordres. Dans les ordres.
Il est devenu l'abbé Alibi,
de la paroisse de Saint-Quelqu'un, on y trouve son
      confessional,
le troisième dans le bas-côté de gauche, côté nord par
      conséquent.
Là il confesse les autres,
mais lui il n'avoue rien.
Même pas qu'il a eu des distractions au cours de sa dernière
      messe,
et qu'il pensait à autre chose.

J'ai écrit ce poème pour corroborer mon ami C. S.
dans la connaissance qu'il a d'un fantôme.

Aux trois quarts du chemin de ma vie,
j'ai écrit ce poème pour l'abbé Alibi,
pour éclairer sa religion.

Mr Alibi has gone into orders. Into orders.
He has become the Abbé Alibi,
of the parish of St. Someone, his confessional can be found there,
    the third one on the left aisle, that is to say on the north side.
There he confesses others,
but himself confesses nothing.
Not even that he suffered distractions in the course of his last
    mass,
and was thinking of something else.

I wrote this poem to strengthen my friend C.S.
in his knowledge of a phantom.

After three quarters of my life's path,
I wrote this poem for the Abbé Alibi,
to illuminate his religion.

L'hiver du Poète

Récit

Les os qui jouaient comme les grains d'un collier, comme
des glaçons sur l'eau,
brusques, se sont refermés,
collés, soudés, une chose compacte
sans plus aucun souvenir du souffle, plus aucun souvenir
    du sang.
Toute rupture s'est vitrifiée, tout ahan
s'étrangle à l'angle de la cristallisation.

Les Ennemis

Nous porterons sur nos épaules ce bloc hostile,
nous descendrons pompeusement ce bloc à sa caverne.
Il y a, dans la caverne, quatre troncs d'arbre tranchés
    à même niveau,
millénairement minéralisés.
Nous poserons ce bloc sur ces quatre bases,
lisses comme le porphyre.
Et comme s'il avait peur, nous hurlerons à son oreille.
Et comme s'il avait soif, nous l'abreuverons d'outrages.
Comme s'il s'amusait, nous lui jouerons la comédie
de celui qui a peur et qui a soif.

Les Filles

Tordez vos cheveux, filles d'Antimoine.
Il ne sait pas que nous l'aimons.
Et vous, palpitez dans nos bras, colombes. Envolez-vous,
    nuages.
Nos destinées sont des baisers évanouis.

The Poet's Winter

Report

The bones that once played like the beads of a necklace, like
bits of ice on water,
snapped shut again,
glued, welded, a compact thing
with no more memory of breath, no more memory of blood.
Every fracture is vitrified, every effort
is strangled in the angle of crystallisation.

Enemies

We'll shoulder this hostile block,
we'll take this block down ceremoniously to its cave.
In the cave there are four tree-trunks cut to the same height,
millenniarily mineralised.
We'll put this block on those four bases,
smooth as porphyry.
And as if it were frightened, we'll yell in its ear.
And as if it were thirsty, we'll spray it with insults.
As if it were enjoying itself, we'll play-act for it
all about someone who's frightened and thirsty.

Daughters

Twist your hair, daughters of Antimony.
He doesn't know we love him.
And you doves, throb in our arms. Fly away, clouds.
Our destinies are kisses that fainted away.

Je lui écris une lettre. Et toi, ma sœur? Le feu
s'éteint. On ne peut plus aimer. Oh! vois donc, ta jupe
s'est toute trempée à la traversée du ruisseau. Silence,
    te dis-je,
silence. Tant d'années ont passé, tant d'années passent
    et passeront.

Les Pensées

À chacun de ses soleils, à chacune de ses musiques,
à chacun de ses cailloux poussés du pied,
s'éveillaient les pensées comme des mouches bruissantes,
comme un adorable hasard de mouches bruissantes,
dans l'estival désordre des présences.
Il s'est retiré de ses pensées comme la richesse
derrière ses fenêtres et la guenille sous son porche,
comme le bonheur dans son adieu.
Même plus une bulle de vide n'éclôt, même plus une de
    ces larmes
que l'âme devine au bord suppliant d'un cil.

1940

Quand la douleur nous berce par les rues provinciales,
au souffle d'un printemps monstrueusement en germe dans
    certains jours d'octobre,
le thym et le cresson somnolent derrière les vitres défuntes
et l'on se demande comment ce monde supportera l'apocalypse.
Trop d'heures de tiédeur et de vieille détresse l'ont affadi.
Ah! qu'il est pâle!
Ses jours se sont succédé comme les jours de fièvre d'un
    vagabond
et la cloche qui sonnait dans sa tête est sourde comme un cri
    de noyé.

I'm writing him a letter. And you, sister? The fire
goes out. No more loving. Oh, look! Your skirt
is all soaked from crossing the stream. Silence, I say,
silence. So many years have passed, so many are passing
    and will pass.

Thoughts

At each of his daybreaks, at each of his tra-las,
at each of his kicked pebbles,
thoughts awoke like buzzing flies,
like a lovable accident of buzzing flies,
in the summertime disorder of things present.
He withdrew from his thoughts like wealth
behind its windows and poverty in its doorway,
like happiness in its goodbye.
Not even a bubble of emptiness bursts, not even one of those tears
that the soul senses on the pleading edge of an eyelash.

1940

When pain cradles us in provincial streets,
at the breath of a spring monstrously sprouting in certain October
    days,
watercress and thyme slumber behind defunct glass panes
and one wonders how this world will come through the
    apocalypse.
Too many hours of dull warmth and old sorrow have smoothed it
    flat.
How pale it is!
Its days have dragged like the days of a vagrant's fever.
The bell that rang in its head is muffled like a drowning cry.

Mémoire Longue

Aventures d'amour par les rues anxieuses
   de l'attente du couvre-feu,
souvenirs parmi les ténèbres périlleuses,
   jeux de spectres silencieux,

vous voilà donc tombés au creux d'un somnambule
   gouffre d'intemporalité.
J'étais libre et puissant dans ce pur crépuscule
   et je me sens déshabité.

J'ai laissé le plus lourd de moi-même à des ombres,
   je leur ai délesté mon cœur
comme ouvre son trésor un navire qui sombre
   en d'amoureuses profondeurs.

Une sphère étrangère a condensé l'haleine
   de tous mes esprits expirés,
insondable pays d'où jamais ne reviennent
   échos, fantômes ni reflets,

Patrie d'exil, cité suspendue dans la fièvre,
   ô plénitude évanouie!
D'un tel épais bonheur ne m'est resté qu'aux lèvres
   la saveur des seins de la nuit.

Mes bras sont retombés de cette étreinte noire.
   Défait, déshérité de moi,
de moi désorienté, je regarde sans voir
   s'anéantir n'importe quoi.

Car tout le lendemain qui m'échoit en partage
   est un rien que multiplie rien
au prix du dénuement et de l'orphelinage
   qui dès lors seront mes vrais biens.

Long Memory

You adventures of love, when the anxious roads
   wait for curfew to end the day,
you memories, games in the perilous shades
   that phantasms silently play,

you've fallen, I see, in the deep sleep-walk
   in the chasm where time stands still.
I was free, I was strong in this pure half-dark,
   now I feel like a home in hell.

I've left to the shadows my heaviest part,
   like a ship that sinks in the sea:
as it pours out its wealth, I unburdened my heart
   to the depths that made love to me.

My spirits have died and their breaths condense
   in the grasp of a foreign sphere,
a land beyond sounding, that never sends
   echoes, phantoms, reflections here,

a homeland of exile, a city that's hung
   (vanished fullness!) in eyes fever-bright.
Of a joy so rich, nothing's left on my tongue
   but the taste of the breasts of night.

My arms fell away from that black embrace.
   Dispossessed of myself, undone,
unhinged, I observe, with a sightless gaze,
   self-destruction of oddments unknown.

For all of the future that falls to my lot
   is a nil that is nil times none,
at the price of privation and parent-loss,
   my real assets from this time on.

Ô nostalgie, ô mes instants, mes grains de sable,
   seuls comptes qui pour moi comptez,
visages disparus, villes méconnaissables,
   je ne suis que ce que j'étais.

Je ne suis que ce flot qui sans cesse reflue
   loin des bras ouverts des grands ports,
plus loin encor, perdu et fier de n'être plus
   que la voix confuse des morts.

O yearning, my moments, my grains of sand,
　　you're the one count that counts for me:
you faces that vanished, you towns out of mind,
　　I'm no more than I used to be.

I am only the wave that keeps ebbing away
　　from great harbours' arms that spread,
still further, and lost, proud merely to be
　　the inchoate voice of the dead.

Si Faible

Si faible et constamment frappé.
Atteint dans son architecture
comme d'une fleur la structure
disjointe sitôt composée.

Il se sépare de ses membres,
il perd images et parfums,
la distance d'août à septembre
et le seuil des plaisirs défunts.

Son axe est disloqué. Le centre
de sa démarche s'engloutit
dans l'aspiration de l'antre
où flottent des ombres transies.

Chair à sa blessure réduite,
chiffre contraint à son erreur,
plus d'autre geste ne l'habite
que le frisson de la terreur.

Vous le reconnaissez: il passe,
il vous parle et vous lui parlez,
et vous croyez voir la grimace
d'un de vos singes familiers.

O touristes, regardez mieux:
il est entré dans la muraille.
Vous n'avez plus devant les yeux
qu'un tombeau de cœur et d'entrailles.

Vous n'avez plus dans la pensée
que, volatile et qui s'étale,
la souvenance consumée
d'une vieille odeur d'hôpital.

Weak, So Weak

Weak, so weak, and taking hits,
injured in his architecture
like a blossom's wounded structure,
formed at once and torn to bits.

See him lose, discard, dismember
self and sights and scents he treasures,
path from August to September,
doorway to departed pleasures.

Out of joint, his central shaft.
See his movement's core engulfed
in the breathing of the cleft
where the quaking shadows waft.

Flesh reduced to mere flesh-wound,
numeral constrained to error,
there's no gesture in him found
but a quivering of terror.

He is known to you: he passes,
you're as affable as he:
you make out the brute grimaces
of an ape you often see.

Tourists, sharpen up your gaze:
he has vanished through the wall.
What is that before your eyes?
Tomb of heart and guts, that's all.

What is that inside your head?
Volatile, and prone to sprawl,
the memory, worn-out and dead,
of an old smell of hospital.

Voyageur, Je Te Conseille

Voyageur, je te conseille de pénétrer dans la ville par la porte de l'Ouest, car cette entrée donne immédiatement accès aux monuments les plus célèbres: le Municipe, la Bourse, le Palais des Horloges, l'Institut de Cartographie. Tu verras aussi les spacieux et vénérables temples: Sainte-Thècle et Saint-Apophtègme, les Augustines, le Saint-Pilier, sans compter le théâtre des Armures, renommé entre toutes les salles de spectacle du monde, et le Marché où la diaprure des fleurs et des poissons forme une fête réjouissante pour les yeux. Là s'ouvre la rue des Cauchemars, avec ses luxueuses boutiques d'objets de piété et les cris de ses marchands de jusquiame et de kaolin. Elle te conduira au port, centre du négoce universel, dont les quais sont animés, nuit et jour, par un grand concours de peuple. Ne manque point d'admirer la Machine Hydraulique, ainsi que la Morgue, établissement réputé et particulièrement prospère. Au demeurant le pré n'est pas loin, où les jeunes gens vident leurs querelles d'honneur. Mais surtout promène-toi sur les planches de la petite rade où les galants et les muguets proposent à leurs belles des promenades en chaloupe. Ces gens de la meilleure société ne craignent point de se mêler en ces lieux à une populace de pêcheurs, de mariniers et de truculents tire-laine: au contraire, ils semblent y éprouver un vif plaisir. Suis leur exemple et engage-toi d'un pas désinvolte dans ce labyrinthe de rues grouillantes, et derrière le chevet d'une église curieuse et assez ancienne qu'on appelle la Canonique, tu verras apparaître la maison que, sur ce plan, j'ai marquée d'une croix. Frappe à la porte, entre, suis le corridor, et au fond de la dernière pièce reconnais ton plus cher et triste souvenir. Personne ne t'aura vu entrer, personne ne te verra sortir. Personne jamais n'entre dans cette maison ni n'en sort, et il n'y a pas de voisins. Je t'avertis qu'à deux pas tu trouveras la meilleure taverne du coin. Le vin y est excellent. Tu dis que tu ne bois plus? Que la moindre goutte de vin te fait mal, très mal, ruine ta santé? Allons, quelle raison te presse de reprendre ton voyage? Qui t'attend, qui t'appelle ailleurs? Qui t'empêche de demeurer désormais dans cette ville fameuse et d'y abréger tes jours?

Traveller, I Advise You

Traveller, I advise you to enter the city at the West Gate, since that entrance gives immediate access to the most famous monuments: the Town Hall, the Stock Exchange, the Palace of Clocks, the Institute of Cartography. You will also see the spacious and venerable places of worship: St. Thecla and St. Apophthegm, the Augustinians, the Holy Pillar, not to mention the Armoury Theatre, renowned among the world's auditoria, and the Market where the multicoloured display of flowers and fishes makes a feast to rejoice the eye. This leads to Nightmare Street, with its luxury boutiques of devotional objects and the cries of its vendors of henbane and china clay. It will bring you to the harbour, the centre of universal trade, its quays bustling night and day with a great throng of people. Don't fail to admire the Hydraulic Machine, and also the Morgue, a respected and outstandingly prosperous establishment. Nearby incidentally is the meadow where the young people settle their disputes of honour. But above all, stroll along the boards of the little jetty where gallants and dandies offer their young ladies a trip in a launch. These high society people are quite unafraid to mix in this area with a populace of fishermen, sailors and aggressive layabouts: on the contrary, they seem to take a keen pleasure in it. Follow their example and stroll into this teeming labyrinth of streets, and behind the apse of a curious and quite ancient church called the Canonical, you will see before you the house which I have marked on this plan with a cross. Knock on the door, go inside, follow the corridor, and at the end of the last room recognise your dearest and saddest memory. No-one will have seen you go in, no-one will see you go out. No-one ever enters or leaves this house, no-one lives nearby. Observe that a step away you will find the best public house in the neighbourhood. Their wine is excellent. You say you don't drink? The smallest drop of wine makes you ill, very ill, ruins your health? Come now, what pressing reason have you to resume your journey? Who is waiting for you, who calls you away? Who prevents you from living here for good in this famous city, and here ending your days?

Tant d'Amour

Tant d'amour n'aurait-il mérité d'autre prix
que lui-même? N'existe-t-il de récompense
en dehors de la propre vertu et du strict
accomplissement? Cette passion, cet immense
offertoire de soi n'eût été que fumée
et jouet de fumée et fétu dans le vent?
Comme l'amour est seul! Et comme tristement
il poursuit son chemin sous d'aveugles regards,
discourant à part soi tel un enfant têtu
et traînant son ballot de choses en retard,
de voyages manqués et de bonheurs perdus!
Amour, chétif amour, triste, triste tristesse,
plaintive plaie au cœur, ne te ferme jamais,
laisse, amour, couler éperdument tes pleurs, laisse
te submerger sans fin, comme un bateau blessé,
l'universel oubli, l'ombre, l'éternité.

Surely So Much Love

Surely so much love would deserve a prize
beyond itself? Is there no recompense
apart from one's own virtue and the strict
accomplishment? That passion, that immense
self-offering, was it no more than smoke,
plaything of smoke, and chaff before the wind?
Love is so solitary. See him find
his dreary way amid unseeing glances,
muttering loudly like a stubborn child,
dragging his bag of halts and hesitancies,
lost happinesses, voyages that failed!
Love, wilful love, sorrowful sad sad sorrow,
the heart's complaining wound, oh never close!
Love, weep your oceans: let them drown and swallow
you down for ever like a stricken vessel:
eternal shade, oblivion universal.

Plaintes de Didon

Les oiseaux de mon roc s'allègent et s'enflamment,
de mes seins éperdus emportant l'ample cri
vertical, mais à qui le frisson plat des lames
oppose un horizon d'implacable mépris.

Ravisseur de pensées, accapareur de graines
mortes avant l'explosion de leurs jardins,
où donc as-tu couru cacher mes ombres vaines?
Quel prix espères-tu d'un si piteux larcin?

Quel antre, quel palais à ce rapt dérisoire
offriront un accueil d'hyperboles gonflé?
Et toi, sentiras-tu, dans le fort de ta gloire,
mon souffle, entre tes doigts, un peu plus expirer?

J'étais large et formée pour de vastes empreintes,
ainsi qu'une montagne étendue sur le dos.
Tu n'auras retiré de moi qu'une âme éteinte
pour me laisser déserte et creusée jusqu'aux os.

Va donc, ce n'est pas moi que je plains, mais tes charmes
qui n'ont pu te servir qu'à ce double forfait.
Tourne en vain contre toi de si stupides armes:
tu ne saurais non plus toi-même t'abuser.

Voleur de rien, trompeur pour rire, assez, ne lève
plus désormais le moindre cil. Retiens ton sang.
Ne laisse plus un son s'effiler de tes lèvres,
ne laisse plus ton nom s'échapper dans le vent.

Dido's Reproaches

My cliff-birds lightly fly, flare up like light,
carry the loud cries of this heart in hell
upwards. Across, my hate without respite
spreads on the water's horizontal swell.

Rapist of thoughts, and profiteer in seed
that died before the fields burst into leaf,
where did you run to hide my futile shade?
What payoff looms for such a paltry thief?

What palace, or what cave, will recompense
this tawdry rape with rapturous acclaim?
Safe in your glory's fortress, will you sense
my spirit in your hands, a guttering flame?

I was large, fashioned to be amply pressed,
mountainous, on my back, a mass of stone.
You only took my dead soul from my breast:
left me, deserted, hollowed to the bone.

Go! I don't care. A pity that your charms
served you for nothing but this shameful double.
Insult yourself! A half-baked feat of arms:
you couldn't even get yourself in trouble.

Thief of nought, cheat for nought! give over now:
don't let your lips emit another sound.
Hold your blood in; don't even twitch your brow;
don't let your name float freely on the wind.

Chaque soir, sur ces mers où des fables nouvelles
vont suivre celles-là dont tu me séduisis,
une île surgira, toujours la même et telle
que tes yeux par la mort se sentiront saisis.

Une île blanche et de structure funéraire,
tendue de trous béants, de gestes insensés,
de cordes et de plis: un chant devenu pierre.
Et ta nef, à son tour, flottera pétrifiée.

Each evening on those seas where many a tale
shall follow the seducer's tales you told,
an island shall rear up, and without fail
your eyes shall feel death's bony claws take hold.

An island, white, and built as if to mourn:
ropes, folds, mad gestures; long holes yawning wide;
a song that turned to stone; and, in its turn,
your ship shall float there, and be petrified.

Enfants Perdus

N'ayant jamais rien demandé,
pas même à vivre,
la jeune Psella passe pour insensible.
On a observé qu'elle n'avait cure
ni du guerrier Biloc ni du notaire Chéradame,
pas plus que d'aucun galant du clan de l'Esturgeon.
Mais durant de soudaines absences
elle se revoit blottie au creux d'un bloc de neige,
entre la louve et la renarde,
si vieilles toutes deux et pleines d'expérience.
Ses compagnes ne sont pas moins étranges,
qui se content des secrets à l'oreille
dans un argot dévergondé.
Les volubilis ont également leurs histoires, et les crocus,
et le chien Spilidore,
et les hommes eux-mêmes,
le cuisinier Crégon et le magistrat Hahach,
et le vieil eunuque Balomphe qui n'a pas toujours été eunuque
et se souvient de ses quatorze fils.
Les dieux aussi, dans leurs courses,
laissent tomber des enfants nostalgiques
et qui ont bien du mal à s'y faire!
Chacun se demande d'où lui vient
cette façon de tenir sa fourchette
et ce mystérieux élan au jarret, et cette impuissance
à prendre au sérieux les plus graves problèmes,
ce goût d'eau salée dans la bouche, cette envie de mourir,
cette indéfinissable envie de mourir,
de mourir encore plus, de mourir encore mieux,
cette divine envie de mourir.
Il dépose des billets au rebord des fenêtres
et pendant vingt ans attend la réponse,
il s'engage dans les armées impériales

Lost Children

She has never asked for anything,
not even to be alive,
so the girl Psella is considered unfeeling.
It is noted that she cared for neither
the warrior Biloc nor the notary Cheradamus,
nor any gallant of the clan Sturgeon.
But during sudden absences
she is seen cowering in a hollow pile of snow,
between vixen and she-wolf,
both so old and experienced.
Her companions are no less peculiar,
whispering secrets in each other's ears
in a shameless jargon.
The bindweeds too have their stories, and the crocuses,
and the dog Spilidor,
and even the human beings,
the cook Cregon and the magistrate Hahash,
and the old eunuch Balomphus who wasn't always a eunuch
and remembers his fourteen sons.
The gods too, go about their business,
spawning children of nostalgia
who find this quite hard to handle!
They all wonder where they picked up
that way of holding a fork,
that mysterious swing to their stride, that inability
to be serious about the gravest problems,
that salt-water taste in the mouth, that desire to die,
that indefinable desire to die,
to die even more, to die even better,
that divine desire to die.
He puts messages on window-sills
and waits twenty years for the answer,
he joins the imperial armies

et reste muet quand son lieutenant l'interroge.
J'ai connu la vierge Mizraïr, que sa mère battait
à coups de baguette de coudrier
pour lui faire avouer qui lui avait donné ce collier
    d'escarboucles,
mais elle ne le disait pas, n'en sachant rien,
et se contentait de remuer la tête de droite et de gauche
avec des yeux hagards et de rauques gémissements.
Elle revenait de la fontaine, son linge sous le bras.
Elle ne savait pas, elle ne savait pas.
J'ai beaucoup connu cette vierge bizarre:
à moi non plus elle n'a jamais rien raconté,
et j'ai été l'ami de son frère aux oreilles de léopard,
qui attrapait les alouettes au vol
et se nourrissait de scarabées
sans jamais dire le pourquoi ni le comment.
Il fut successivement peseur de choux et peseur d'âmes,
puis, nommé amiral de la flotte, remporta
la célèbre victoire du cap Céleste
sous le proconsulat d'Abénobar.
Si, pardon, une seule fois,
une seule fois, je me souviens,
il m'a fait part de l'une de ses pensées,
mais si chétive, mais toute tremblante,
une pensée par rapport au soleil,
ou à un astre qu'il appelait ainsi
et qui tournait dans sa mémoire
comme un char aux essieux grinçants.
Je me souviens: à ce même instant passait sur la route
un raccommodeur de vieilles pluies et d'éclairs cassés
qui soufflait dans sa trompette.
Nous lui avons demandé notre chemin, mais comment
    l'aurait-il pu dire
puisqu'il avait perdu le sien?
Mais vous, voyons, n'avez-vous jamais rencontré

and says nothing, when his officer questions him.
I knew the virgin Mizraïr, whose mother beat her
with a hazel switch
to make her confess who had given her the necklace of carbuncles,
but she didn't say, as she didn't know,
and merely moved her head to left and right
with haggard eyes and raucous groans.
She was coming back from the fountain, her washing under her
 arm.
She didn't know, she didn't know.
I knew this peculiar virgin quite well:
she never told me anything either,
and I was a friend of her brother who had leopard's ears,
who caught skylarks on the wing
and fed on scarabs
with never a why or a how.
He went from weighing cabbages to weighing souls,
then he was named admiral of the fleet, and won
the famous victory of Cape Celeste
in the proconsulship of Abenobar.
Oh yes, my mistake, just once,
just once, I remember,
he did share one of his thoughts with me,
but it was so abject, all tremulous,
a thought compared to the sun,
or a star, that's what he called it,
and it churned in his memory
like a tank with grinding axles.
I remember! Coming down the road at that moment
was a mender of old rain-showers and broken lightning
blowing a trumpet.
We asked him the way, but how could he have told us,
having lost his own?
But, you, look here, did you never meet

une demoiselle Salcipède
que la chanson de la machine à coudre faisait pleurer?
Elle n'avait pour confident que son vieil oncle,
toujours plus vieux,
hallebardier de son état,
et qui, dans sa maison à l'odeur conventuelle,
gardait un coffre de coquillages,
une armoire de costumes de parade,
une horloge à musique,
une lampe à larmes de miel et de sang.
La chronique extérieure déroulait son rouleau
flamboyant, retentissant,
et ne faisait jamais allusion à ces curiosités.
La chronique se déroule, sans fin, le malheur rôde,
et la rivière Narasaga coule,
qui, depuis le dernier traité de paix, s'appelle Gasarana.
Mais les étrangers l'appellent Ko.
Il n'y a qu'elle qui ne sache comment elle s'appelle
et peut-être les amants couchés au fond de la yole
qu'elle emporte en son cours d'azur poli.
Ils se soucient bien de son nom!
Ils parlent d'autre chose,
à peine, si peu,
Ils ne parlent même pas d'autre chose.
Ils ont faim et ils ont peur.

a young lady called Salcipede,
who wept at the song of the sewing-machine?
Her only confidant was her old uncle,
who kept on getting older,
a halberdier by his calling,
who kept, in his house that smelt like a convent,
a chest of shellfish,
a cupboard of parade costumes,
a musical clock,
a lamp of tear-drops of honey and blood.
The chronicle of outside unfurled its scroll,
flamboyant, resounding,
never mentioning these curiosities.
The chronicle unfurls endlessly, misfortune prowls,
And the river Narasaga flows on,
whose name, since the last peace-treaty, is Gasarana.
But foreigners call it Ko.
Everyone knows its name except the river itself
and perhaps the lovers in bed down below in the yawl
which it carries away on its polished azure course.
Much they care about its name!
They talk about something else,
hardly at all, so little,
they don't even talk about something else.
They are hungry and afraid.

Géographie de la France!

Géographie de la France! Le prochain train ne passera que
    dans une heure.
Une heure qu'il faut grignoter aux abords de la gare, sur la
    route sèche et à la terrasse
de ce cabaret qui ne peut offrir que d'écœurantes limonades.
Une heure de lenteur et de minutieuses délices,
et tant de localité dans cette vacance,
et dans cette étroitesse tant de musique et de mémorable
    fortune!
Patience! d'autres heures épaissiront la grange, et te voici,
qui surgis entre les clochers, toi, ville de la détresse et du
    combat,
ma toute belle!
Ah! je puis, dans mes loisirs, me raconter que nulle part
    qu'en toi je n'ai jamais saigné de plus d'amour,
ni connu plus splendide béatitude.
Le bonheur est demeuré là, et il était compact, odorant et
    miraculeux. J'ai repris ma voie,
comme au long d'un rayon qui repart et s'éteint,
mais le bonheur!
Il est demeuré là, ineffable, et alentour le temps éblouissant
    fait ses trous noirs.
Moi, je sais qu'il est là et non ailleurs,
comme un trésor dans un coffre de fer caché par un matelot
    sagace,
et le matelot s'en va tanguant et clignant de l'œil, plus ivre à
    chaque escale,
non plus heureux, mais ivre, et il a bien raison!
Routes, routes, entrées des villes, faubourgs, boutiques,
    boutiques, boutiques, celle-ci, celle-là, défilé infini des
    étalages, sinuosité des rues mystérieuses, la Grand-rue et
    la ruelle des Moines, ô bel échantillon de passementerie!
Encore un peu de cœur au ventre pour ce pays sur la carte!
Les doigts de l'instituteur ont extrait un fer de lance des
    cendres de Montségur,
les fées ont piétiné l'herbe autour du plus gros chêne de la
    forêt de Tronçais,

Atlas of France!

Atlas of France! The next train isn't due for another hour.
An hour to be nibbled away on the station forecourt, the arid
   road and the terrace
of this bar that offers only repulsive lemonades.
An hour of slowness and small-scale pleasures,
so much that's local in this emptiness,
and in this narrowness, so much music, so much memorable
   fortune!
Relax! Other hours will fill up the corn-shed, and here you are,
rearing up amid the belfries, you, city of sorrow and battle,
my beauty!
Ah! I can recall at leisure that nowhere else have I shed more
   of my heart's blood for love,
or known greater bliss.
Happiness lasted there, and it was tight, fragrant,
   miraculous. I resumed my journey,
as if on a light-ray that starts and stops,
but the happiness!
Lingering, indescribable. The dazzle of time makes black
   holes all around it.
I know it's there and nowhere else,
like the treasure a canny sailor hides in an iron chest,
and the sailor goes pitching and rolling, winking his eye, and
   more lit up at every port,
not happier, but lit up, and quite right too!
Roads, roads, ways into cities, suburbs, shops, shops, shops,
   this one, that one, endless window-displays, streets
   mysteriously curving, High Street, Monks Lane, what
   a sampler of fine needlework!
A little more heart in the belly for this country on the map!
The teacher's fingers pulled an iron spear-point from the
   ashes of Montségur,
the fairies trampled the grass round the stoutest oak in the
   forest of Tronçais,

les villages se refaisaient après chaque invasion,
et la vierge des fortifications voyait reparaître à l'horizon
    l'aurore et le chemin de fer.
Vaste regard scrutateur, fidélité, ô capitale, étends
les tentacules de ta vorace souvenance et conserve
le tissu des carrefours, la chaîne des arceaux, la carrière
    des tailloirs,
la poussée basaltique, l'étang de César et le conseil
    municipal,
l'éternité dans la lumière.

the villages revived after every invasion,
the virgin of the fortifications saw daybreak and railways
　　looming on the horizon.
Vast overview, fidelity, O capital city! Stretch out
the tentacles of your devouring memory and preserve
the tissue of intersections, the arcade, the quarry of columns,
the basalt outcrop, Caesar's pool and the municipal council,
eternity in the light.

Mars Émerveillé

Quoi? disait ce guerrier, c'est dans mes bras, Vénus,
que tombe ton destin de beauté souveraine:
tes cheveux nonpareils, ta gorge, tes pieds nus
et le trésor marin que tes cuisses détiennent!

Entre tant de servants du nombre universel,
indiscernables chacun de chacun, pourquoi
celui-ci qui ne répond: moi, qu'au seul appel
de lui-même, sans doute aussi dénommé moi?

Mais, oh! l'obscure voix qui s'aventure ainsi
sous l'armure pareille aux pareilles armures,
quel enfouissement de fol orgueil parmi
la rigoureuse égalité des morts futurs!

Choix de la foudre! Vol frémissant de la bille
tremblant de prononcer son chiffre, et toi, couteau,
aile d'oiseau de mer, qui sinues et scintilles
sur la vaste étendue des cornes de taureaux!

Mon taureau! Noir ou blanc, fils du sort, je t'embrasse.
J'embrasse tout destin par la nuit projeté
et, sur l'autel massif de mon thorax, j'enlace
mon propre chef de mes deux bras de fer noués,

attendant qu'à leur place, adorable mystère,
apparaissent, Vénus, tes bras, fleuve de lait
d'amande douce, odeur condensée de lumière,
collier, bouche d'abîme et de suavité.

Loin de m'y engloutir, j'y trouve ma naissance
et le cercle lustral de mes fonts baptismaux.
J'existe par tes cris, tes extases, tes transes
et c'est pour ma saillie que tu jaillis des flots.

Mars Awestruck

'What!' said the warrior, 'Venus, in my arms
your destiny as sovereign beauty lies.
Bare feet, and throat, your hair's unrivalled charms,
and the sea-treasure guarded by your thighs!

Of all the whole world's interchangeable
obedient servants, madam, tell me why
this one, who answers 'I' to one sole call:
his own, and that itself is surely 'I'.

But, high adventure for this voice, half-heard,
in this plain armour of the armoury!
High pride, in strict equality interred,
plunged among equals who are doomed to die.

Thunder to choose! the bullet's whirring flight
trembles to speak its number, and the blade,
wing of a seabird, sinuously bright,
thrusts through wide horns of bulls its estocade.

My bull of fate! White, black, in my embrace!
I grasp the fate thrust on me by the night,
and on my breast's great altar I enlace
my head, in my two arms of iron held tight,

till in their place, mysterious, marvellous,
Venus, your arms appear, soft stream of milk
of almonds, sweet quintessence luminous,
necklace, and mouth abyssal, smooth as silk.

I'm not submerged, but find my birth in this,
find my baptismal springs, my lustral home,
exist in your cries, trances, ecstasies.
To mate with me you spurted from the foam.

Et toi, n'est-ce étonnant que de tant de déesses
et de nymphes des bois, des prairies, des rochers,
ce soit toi qui, sitôt que je dise: maîtresse,
t'encoures sur mon cœur ton visage cacher?

J'écarte tes cheveux, j'écarte tes paupières,
je te regarde jusqu'au fond de ton regard.
Non, je ne connaîtrai jamais d'heure dernière
et dans l'éternité je mets tout notre espoir.

Strange that of all those goddesses, divine
nymphs of the woods, the fields, the mountain-crest,
you are the one, when I say: mistress mine,
who runs to hide her forehead in my breast!

I brush aside your lashes and your hair,
gaze deep into the chasms of your gaze.
No, I shall never know a final hour:
I store up all our hope in endless days.'

Glorieuse Romería

à Jorge Guillén

Peuples et fleuves rassemblés,
terres en foule confluantes,
bateaux, drapeaux, houle des blés
se ruent à la chose évidente.

Chanter d'azur, je te salue
et vous, ensoleillé courir,
aspirer une aurore nue,
danser d'écume et de saphir,

et solennels manger et boire!
Ô gestes, chers actes sacrés,
quels parements ostentatoires
n'avez-vous enfin mérités?

Et les feuillages, les feuillages,
qu'ils bruissent, multipliés
depuis les fonds des paysages
jusque sur les fronts des bergers!

Mais les feuillages! les subtiles
folioles de l'été fort,
vives plus qu'un frisson de cils
et nombreuses plus que les morts!

Richesse infernale, feuillages,
rameaux d'or, grand-œuvre de l'art
qui va de l'œuf noir au plumage
et des racines au regard!

Sous sa coupe quelle main bleue
recompose, éparses parcelles,
toutes les énergies du lieu
et les ordonne à sa tutelle?

Glorious Romería

to Jorge Guillén

Peoples and rivers assembled,
countries all confluent,
banners and boats and corn-swell
haste to the shining event.

Song of deep blue, I salute you,
you, running-race in the sun,
dancing in foam and sapphire,
breathing a naked dawn,

you, solemn feasts and libations!
Actions and rituals too:
all the refined ostentations
must be, already, your due.

And all the leaves on the branches,
may they redouble their noise,
from the far-off rustic marches
to the brows of shepherd-boys!

Ah but the foliage! The subtle
leaves of the summer's firm tread,
lively as lashes that flutter,
leaves that outnumber the dead!

Wealth subterranean, foliage:
golden boughs, artistry too,
from the black egg to the plumage,
from the dark roots into view.

In the vault what azure hand
gleans the pieces scattered there,
all the forces of the land,
marshals them into its care?

Quelle espérance l'horizon
circulaire tient embrassée
pour l'assourdissant unisson
d'une merveilleuse journée?

Je dis, à cette heure et céans,
que le règne de la tendresse
est venu. Je dis qu'il suspend
le déclin de toute jeunesse.

Je dis perdus les souvenirs,
les avenirs, les éphémères
dans un présent sans nul finir,
comme des pensées dans la mer,

comme des pensées pérégrines,
mes pensées enfin à leur but:
l'illustre immanence marine
d'un absolu diamant brut.

Jeux et joies, pleurs de joie, extase,
tête en fête, vermeil séjour,
cœurs en accord au cœur qu'embrase
la totalité de l'amour!

Les enfants et les jeunes filles,
imitant le sort des oiseaux,
se reconnaissent leur famille
dans le spectacle du ruisseau.

Chaque brindille, chaque pierre,
chaque son qui se veut chanté,
chaque main, chaque œil énumère
ses éperdues proximités.

Is there hope within the ring,
in the far horizon's circle,
for the single deafening
concert-note of one day's miracle?

I declare to you today
that the reign of tenderness
is at hand. It halts, I say,
the decline of youthfulness:

and all things ephemeral,
memories, futures, cease to be,
lost in the perennial
present, sunk like thoughts at sea:

roving thoughts in transience,
thoughts of mine that reach their end,
sea's illustrious immanence,
purest uncut diamond.

Games, joys, tears of joy, and blisses,
head's red-letter holidays,
hearts in tune with hearts that kisses,
in love's fullness, set ablaze!

Children and young girls take after
birds who frolic on the wing,
in the sight of running water
recognise their kith and kin.

Every sprig and every stone,
every sound where music lives,
every hand and eye, as one,
counts its lovestruck relatives.

Un bourdon d'abeilles irise
la béate sieste des gueux.
Le sang des vins et des cerises
débouche en soupirs langoureux.

L'œillet, la menthe, l'hyacinthe,
le basilic, le romarin,
tirent l'âme à l'ultime pointe
de la stridence des parfums.

Ô mes aimées, sur vos épaules
renversez la nuque pour voir
vos rires de colombes folles
monter vers l'immense ostensoir.

Asseyons-nous dans l'herbe. L'heure
approche où la magicienne
va teindre d'étranges couleurs
notre demeure souveraine.

J'entends tinter les clefs du soir.
L'air se fait tendre, la peau douce.
Les fraîches eaux du reposoir
se répandent parmi la mousse.

Encore plus sacramentel
que la lumière du matin,
un vaste éventail, d'un coup d'ailes,
va fondre en rêves le distinct.

Voici donc l'extrême message:
pour enchanter la nuit sachez
que nous avons dans nos villages
de fort experts artificiers.

Hum of bees, siesta-flood,
dapples beggars' reveries;
blood of wines and cherry-blood
all pour out in languid sighs.

Hyacinth, carnation, mint,
rosemary, and basil press
the soul to the furthest point
of their scents' assertiveness.

O my darlings, tilt your heads
on your shoulders and espy
how your mad-dove laughter spreads
to the monstrance of the sky.

Here is grass, we'll sit and pause.
The enchantress comes to stain,
presently, with wondrous hues,
our abode, our sovereign

dwelling. Hear the keys of dusk!
Air grows tender, soft the skin.
Rest, be thankful. See the moss:
blest, cool water seeping in.

Still more sacramental than
sunlight's early-morning beam,
wing-beat of a giant fan
melts distinctness into dream.

Here then is the final message.
To enchant the night, know this:
we can boast in any village
fireworks staged with artifice.

Les astres ne sont nos seuls maîtres
ni les nuées ni l'œil de Dieu,
ni rien de ce que fait paraître
quelque histrion prestigieux.

Tant d'admirables influences,
si nous en sommes pénétrés,
c'est pour, à leur tour, nos puissances,
leur inspirer de se montrer.

« Mes beaux enfants, nous dit Nature,
mon intime et tenace loi,
c'est que vous couriez l'aventure
de rivaliser avec moi. »

À sortilège sortilège
plus volage et plus éclatant!
Nos étoiles, à nous, s'allègent
du piège du funèbre aimant.

Nos esprits, égalant au ciel
le feu dont ils sont possédés,
tracent, d'un concours d'étincelles,
une figure de ballet,

une figure intelligente,
ô les dames de mes pensées,
mes suaves tailles ployantes,
mes assises à mes côtés!

Du fond de l'ombre qui s'est faite
sur la rotondité du jour,
contemplons atteindre à son faîte
la conjonction des amours.

Fuse le génie de la terre!
Qu'il se dessine, exterminé,
or jailli, mort forgée, poussière
d'incandescente éternité.

We have more than stars to teach us,
more than clouds and heaven's eye,
we have more than any specious
histrionic trickery.

May such splendid influences
penetrate us through and through,
rouse in turn our competences,
set them surging into view.

Hark, my bonny brood, says Nature,
to my deep and firm decree:
dare to launch on this adventure,
matching stroke for stroke with me.

Sorcery on sorcery,
Brilliant, unpredictable!
Now our stars have shaken free
of the dismal magnet's thrall.

Our spirits, matching to the sky
the fire of their obeisance,
in the crowd of sparks that fly
trace a figure of the dance:

trace a figure that is wise,
O you ladies in my head,
lovely pliant presences
close beside me billeted.

Deep in shade that makes its move
on the day's rotundity,
let us watch conjoining love
reach its zenith in the sky.

Spirit of the earth, diffused!
Let it loom, and cease to be:
gold in spate, death fashioned, dust
of white heat's eternity.

Other Poems: Notes

'**A Rose that was Drowning**' is the first poem of *The Rose and the Wine*, the sequence of over thirty generally optimistic poems which Cassou wrote in 1940-41, before his imprisonment and brush with death. He added lengthy commentaries before publishing them in 1952. Many of the poems have appeared in English in *33 Sonnets and Other Poems*, from the present translator, with the French alongside.

'**Triumph**' is dated 'Mauzac 1943 to Paris 1947'. Mauzac was a detention camp where Cassou served part of his sentence. The poem starts bleakly but ends with a consoling vision, the armies of the sick being healed by the power of love. Cassou's rhyme-scheme looks at first to be the *terza rima*, the endless chain of triple rhymes that took Dante from hell through purgatory to paradise: but that is used only at the end, the first half of the poem being rhymed in self-contained sestets. Triple rhymes are hard in French, harder in English, so this translation is less regularly rhymed than the original. The simple rhymes in the late stanzas of the English make perhaps for lightness and lift.

The translator has to translate this poem without knowing what it means. *The Madness of Amadis* by contrast is a lucid narrative, therefore easy to paraphrase, which in turn makes triple rhyme feasible in every stanza. *Triumph* is quite obscure, so the translator has stayed closer to the wording of the original.

'**Schist Country**'. The child is like the Greco-Egyptian deity Harpocrates, who, with a finger on his lips, enjoins a philosophical silence.

'**Pride, Secret Child**'. Compare Sonnet XXV, line 8: 'My proud and pensive face...'

'**Mr Alibi**'. This poem was translated into German by the Dada artist, Hans/Jean Arp. The dedicatee C.S. is possibly Camille Soula, Cassou's fellow-resistant, physiologist, friend of Giraudoux, commentator on Mallarmé. 'His friends adored him', wrote Cassou in *Une Vie pour la Liberté*, 1981, 'for his truculent eloquence and fiery opinions, extravagant demeanour and total originality'.

'**1940**'. A vagrant's fever. Compare Cassou's 'The Day': 'The day burnt like a sick man's bed'. Also his Sonnet XIV: 'That drifter at our fire one windy night,/ Trying to warm her damaged hands: my word...'

'Long Memory' (1952). Cassou uses this metre, or similar, for some of his more desolate visions: 'Sadness of the Distorting Mirror', *'Chez Moi'* (1960, more consoling), 'The Day'.

'Weak, So Weak' (1947). In 'A Rose that was Drowning' the flower dissolves in a delicious surrender: but not here.

'Dido's Reproaches' (1950). Dido curses her lover, the Trojan Aeneas. He is leaving her and her city of Carthage, where he has been rescued and welcomed, to fulfil instead his destiny as the founder of Rome. In Virgil's words (*Æneid IV*):

> i, sequere Italiam ventis, pete regna per undas.
> spero equidem mediis, si quid pia numina possunt,
> supplicia hausurum scopulis et nomine Dido
> saepe vocaturum. sequar atris ignibus absens:
> et, cum frigida mors anima seduxerit artus,
> omnibus umbra locis adero. dabis, improbe, poenas.
> audiam et haec Manis veniet mihi fama sub imos.

Go, chase Italy on the winds, look for kingdoms amid the waves. Yes, if the pious gods have power, I hope you run on the rocks, and there swallow your punishment, calling and calling Dido's name. Absent, I shall pursue you with black fires: and when cold death has parted body from spirit, I shall haunt you, everywhere. Wrongdoer, you shall pay the penalty. I shall hear of it: in the deepest underworld, the rumour will reach me.

Dido's curse is not merely personal but calls down the calamity of war on the two nations. Rome and Carthage fought three times:

> litora litoribus contraria, fluctibus undas
> imprecor, arma armis: pugnent ipsique nepotesque.
> *This I invoke: shores against shores, waves against waves,*
> *arms against arms: war for themselves, war for their seed.*

'Atlas of France!' Montségur is the fortress, perched in the Pyrenean foothills, where in 1243-4 the Cathar defenders resisted central authority, to the death; also a prehistoric site. Its link with the Holy Grail legend was famous long before the Second World War.

The Forest of Tronçais is in the department of Allier, in the Auvergne. The tallest oak (now 41m) in the Colbert Stand was named in honour of Pétain in 1940, then of Gabriel Péri, and is now called the Resistance Oak.

Here is Cassou on the Troubadours:

'A kingdom submerged, an Atlantis, a fable: such, it seems, is the civilisation of Oc. Certainly since the cataclysm the southern provinces have constantly contributed to the history and genius of France, and done so by their own character: traced easily enough, but more fruitfully if we knew more about its origins, and about the century when it showed off all its singular brilliance. The fires of Oc still shine, but sadly we cannot reach their base, the mysterious sparkling treasure sunk deep in the Ariège.

'Many a knight-errant has thrilled to this quest of the Grail of Montségur. Their searches, theories, surmises are a delight, and in this lair or that, they have managed to hold the chimera at bay... We know the civilisation of Oc has titles of nobility. It was the first civilisation of France: a useful and prolific fact to consider. When the lands north of the Loire were still lurching into a barbaric dawn, when the wonders of the Gothic were not yet proclaimed, Toulouse was the capital of a refined society. The first cathedrals were rearing up in Romanesque garb; the forgotten art of sculpting the human form was rising again from the shadows, yielding to the curves of tympanum and squinch, breaking free of the wall-surface, the angle of the capital, the functional necessity of columns: the poignant stuttering of a language lost and recovered. Another invention, no less sublime than sculpture, was going forward in this land: the invention of poetry.

'The Troubadours' poetry is born of a dual system, both moral and aesthetic, the two becoming identical in a single search for asceticism. In the forms and rules of *trobar clus*, closed poetry, there is a rigour akin to spiritual rigour. The diction is meagre, codified, regulated, ritual, reduced to a cipher; the prosody is strict and leads to the most difficult combinations of words; this whole hermetic and monotone construction brings a mystical exercise under a no less severe command. There is a limited number of attitudes and situations into which the subject is constrained by an inaccessible object. Love is forbidden from the outset, and that is the rule and the benefit. Love is held captive by a jealous and all-powerful husband – usually the same liege lord who is the poet's patron – love is adulterous and therefore policed, symbolic, conventional, ritual and courtly; love is contradictory and therefore chaste – *d'amor mou castitatz*, of love comes chastity, Montanhagol declares. Love is distant

– Jaufre Rudel's *amor de lonh* – love is found in absence, in separation, in death, and the poet applies his pleading to the various steps on the mental path imposed by his confinement. These moments are called desire, regret, joy in service, desolation. A whole casuistry is parlayed into themes that may be melancholy, patient, ecstatic or anguished. There are set categories under which various emotions will be possible, various utterances permitted. The poet and his song are located by reference to a dominant example which persists as his idea and his reason. *Dousa res ben ensenhada*, sighs Bernard de Ventadour. The lady, the *domna*, is well *enseignée*, that is, she embodies *sen*, the Catalan *seny*: good sense, wit and wisdom. She is exalted, the centre of highest choice, the target of volition, the pitch of intellect, a queen elected and proclaimed, an image exquisite and resolved, the name and sign of honour, arousing the most ardent lyrical hyperbolæ. And just as she can be praised only in metre and idiom that bristle with difficulties, so too she grants the heart only an array of insoluble contradictions. So it is that Arnaud Daniel, the most glorious and subtle of the masters of *trobar clus*, who is eulogised by Dante, appears to us only as the fixed point of impossibility, the ultimate victim, who lives by not living and dies by not dying:

Je suis Arnaud qui amasse la brise,   *I am Arnaud who heaps up the breeze*,
me sers du bœuf à la chasse du lièvre,   *I use the ox when I hunt the hare*,
et vais nageant à rebrousse-marée.   *And I go swimming against the tide.*

'But the name of Love is not invoked in vain. And this Love, whose *leys* or laws were to end up as mere rules of rhetoric in Occitania's decay, this Love is still love, for all of that. And these different lyrical possibilities, set in the framework of a rigorous mythico-aesthetic doctrine, finally reveal themselves to us as situations that every man of flesh and blood experiences, in which his very real feelings are expressed. In Troubadour poetry, however general it may seem and however much it may resemble a liturgy, we hear particular human voices and accents, a beating heart, a spirited melody, the elegy of a love lived out. The mystery takes flesh, is profaned, unveiled. Delicious music is conjured: and among the genres these poets cultivated, we are especially touched by the *aubes*, the Dawns, which reflect one of Love's ceremonies, one of its sacred comedies: the moment when the nocturnal lovers, to the guilty joy of their sentry at his look-out post, refuse to heed his alarm, cling to their ecstasy, resist cruel dawn with an illicit, improbable, unreal prolonging of the infinite shades. An immeasurably rich theme, that of Romeo and Juliet in the night, that on which Guiraut de Borneil composed one of the most marvellous poems of any literature:

...Beau doux ami, je suis en si doux lieu
Que je voudrais qu'il ne fût jamais jour.
Du monde entier je tiens la plus aimable
Entre mes bras; aussi ne prise guère
Le fol jaloux ni l'aube.

...My fair sweet friend, I am in place so sweet
That I would wish the day might never come.
Of all the world I hold the dearest one
Here in my arms; so I do not regard
The jealous fool, nor dawn.

'Troubadour poetry, then, cannot be taken for a mere curiosity reserved for fanciers of chinoiserie. Despite the battle of Muret and the expansion of *la langue d'oil* and its triumph over *la langue d'oc*, the Troubadour spirit has breathed on the world: it inspired the *dolce stil nuovo*, Dante and Petrarch, and the Catalans, notably the two famous 15th-century Valencians, Jordi de Sant Jordi and Auzias March. And it is found again, alive in many a current and talent of our literature, because in the face of romanticism it represents one of poetry's perennial attitudes, that of meeting emotion with a system, and combining, as if with a grid and a number, all the heart's vicissitudes and dramas into an emblematic, a table of metaphors, or some other order, sum, or linguistic method; to achieve the most passionate outpourings only by way of recompense for a doctrine or a discipline.'

From *Parti Pris: Essais et Colloques*, Albin Michel, 1964.

'Mars Awestruck'. (1952.) The Goddess of Love receives her finest homage in Latin poetry from Lucretius, at the very opening of his great scientific and philosophical work *De Rerum Natura*, 'On The Nature Of Matter'. *Aeneadum genetrix, hominum divomque voluptas, / alma Venus...* She causes the birth of all creatures, dispels winds and clouds, makes the flowers grow, calms the sea and sky, causes birds and beasts to mate in spring, fills all nature with joy and love. She can lull the grim weapons of war on land and sea, bring peace to mankind.

nam tu sola potes tranquilla pace iuvare
mortalis, quoniam belli fera moenera Mavors
armipotens regit, in gremium qui saepe tuum se
reiicit aeterno devictus vulnere amoris,
atque ita suspiciens tereti cervice reposta

pascit amore avidos inhians in te, dea, visus
eque tuo pendet resupini spiritus ore.
hunc tu, diva, tuo recubantem corpore sancto
circum fusa super, suavis ex ore loquellas
funde petens placidam Romanis, incluta, pacem.

*For only you can aid mankind with tranquil peace. For Mars the war-god
has often lain back in your lap, smitten by love's eternal wound: with neck
stretched back, he looks up, and browses on love, supine, his eyes devouring
you, his breath hanging from your lips. Goddess, draped over him as he
reclines on your sacred body, glorious one: with winning words, ask for the
Romans to have rest and peace.'*

Venus, being the mother of Aeneas by the mortal Anchises, is also
the supposed ancestor of Julius Caesar and his adopted son and heir,
Augustus. At the end of Ovid's *Metamorphoses* it emerges that, for all her
pleading, Julius Caesar could not be saved. She places him as a god among
the stars, to witness the glory of his still greater son.

Venus and Mars are illicit lovers. She is married to the lame artificer-
god, Vulcan, who is about to trap the guilty pair in a metal net... Lustration
is the motion of the priests of Mars, a going round from place to place,
sometimes in a more earthy sense; also ritual purification by water. The
estocade is the single sword-thrust in the bullring, the 'moment of truth': a
rare word in English. Vita Sackville-West uses it in her poem *The Garden*,
as the Battle of Britain rages above Sissinghurst. Jean Cassou's love-poem
explores the psychology of mutual conquest.

'Glorious Romería'. Romería in Spanish (from *romero*, the aromatic
shrub rosemary, in Latin *ros marinum*, sea-dew) means properly a joyful
pilgrimage of many people converging for a rural festival. The *reposoir*
'resting-place' is in this context also a wayside altar. Like 'And There Was
Light' in Cassou's earlier sequence *The Rose and the Wine*, this poem
dated 1953 expresses a visionary joy.

A Short Bibliography

Cassou's poetry
Trente-trois Sonnets Composés au Secret. Éditions de Minuit, Paris, 1944, and Éditions de la Baconnière, Neuchâtel, 1946.
Oeuvre Lyrique/Das Lyrische Werk, 2 vols. Erker, St Gallen, 1971.
Trente-trois Sonnets Composés au Secret, La Rose et le Vin, La Folie d'Amadis: Éditions Gallimard, 1995. Introduction by Florence de Lussy.

Cassou's poetry in translation
Sonette aus dem Kerker: a German version of the 33 Sonnets by Franz von Rexroth. Bilingual edition. Limes Verlag, Wiesbaden, 1957.
Das Lyrische Werk, Erker, 1971, see above: his collected poems all with German versions in a bilingual edition. Many translators, including Hans/Jean Arp, the Dada poet and sculptor. The 33 Sonnets are translated by Max Rieple; other rhymed poems by Hannelise Hinderberger.
Nine Sonnets, transl. Jacqueline Kiang. Modern Poetry in Translation, new series, nos. 1(1992) and 16 (2000).
33 Sonnets of the Resistance and Other Poems, transl. Timothy Adès. Arc Publications, 2002. Original introduction by Louis Aragon, and new introduction by Alistair Elliot.
Five Poems, transl. Timothy Adès. Translation and Literature, Edinburgh University Press, vol. 6, part 2, 1997.
From A Condemned Cell: the 33 Sonnets translated by Harry Guest. Limited edition, bilingual, with notes. itinerant press, 2008.
Music: two sonnets set by Manuel Rosenthal, four by Henri Dutilleux.

Exhibition Catalogue: Jean Cassou, un Musée Imaginé.
Bibliothèque Nationale de France / Centre Georges Pompidou, 1995. A comprehensive document of Cassou's life and career. 251 pages, with numerous fine essays, quotations, pictures, etc.

Commentaries and Reviews
Pierre Georgel in Les Poètes d'Aujourd'hui, Seghers, 1967.
Will Stone in The Times Literary Supplement, 19.9.2003.
Anthony Rudolf in Stand, vol. 5, no. 3, 2004.
John Pilling in Poetry Nation Review, Nov/Dec 2004.
W.S. Milne in Agenda, vol. 40, no. 4, 2004.

The Translator

Timothy Adès, born 1941 in Surrey, learnt classical verse composition at school, took a degree in classics and studied international business management. He translates poetry especially with rhyme and metre. He won the Premio Valle-Inclán Prize, 2001, for *Homer in Cuernavaca* by Alfonso Reyes, and the John Dryden Prize, 2003, for Victor Hugo's poems *Moscow, Waterloo, St Helena*, and BCLA/BCLT awards for Cassou's *33 Sonnets* and for *Against the Grain* by Robert Desnos. In 2002 Victor Hugo's *How to be a Grandfather* appeared from Hearing Eye, and Cassou's *33 Sonnets and Other Poems* from Arc. Translations of thirty-five poems by Bertolt Brecht have appeared, and a volume of Robert Desnos is forthcoming. Timothy Adès selected these poems of Cassou, and wrote the introduction, notes and other translations in this volume.

Foreword

Harry Guest was born in Penarth in 1932. He read Modern Languages at Cambridge before beginning a career as a teacher in schools and universities in Japan and England. An Honorary Research Fellow at the University of Exeter, he has published three novels, and his many fine collections of poetry have been translated into several languages. He himself chose and translated *Postwar Japanese Poetry* (a Penguin book) and *The Distance, The Shadows,* an anthology of poetry by Victor Hugo. *A Puzzling Harvest* is a recent collection of his own poems.

The Artist

Christopher Le Brun RA, born 1951 in Portsmouth, studied at the Slade and at Chelsea. His many major credits include Contemporary Voices, New York 2005. A former trustee of the Tate and the National Gallery, and a trustee of the Prince's Drawing School, he is on the Council of the Royal Academy, and in 2000 became its first Professor of Drawing.